KENDAL - WINDERME

AMBLESIDE · GRASMERE · STAVELEY

G000298760

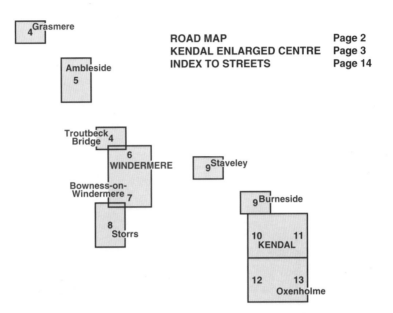

ROAD MAP Page 2
KENDAL ENLARGED CENTRE Page 3

4 Grasmere

Ambleside
5

Troutbeck
Bridge 4

6
WINDERMERE

9 Staveley

Bowness-on-
Windermere 7

9 Burneside

8
Storrs

10   11
KENDAL

12   13
Oxenholme

Every effort has been made to verify
the accuracy of information in this
book but the publishers cannot accept
responsibility for expense or loss
caused by an error or omission.
Information that will be of assistance
to the user of the maps will be welcomed.

The representation on these maps of a
road, track or path is no evidence of the
existence of a right of way.

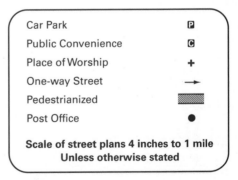

Car Park	🅿
Public Convenience	🅲
Place of Worship	+
One-way Street	→
Pedestrianized	▨
Post Office	●

**Scale of street plans 4 inches to 1 mile
Unless otherwise stated**

Street plans prepared and published by ESTATE PUBLICATIONS, Bridewell House,
TENTERDEN, KENT, and based upon the ORDNANCE SURVEY mapping with the permission
of The Controller of H. M. Stationery Office.

The Publishers acknowledge the co-operation of the local authorities
of towns represented in this atlas.

© Estate Publications 610 A   ISBN 1 84192 039 8   © Crown Copyright 398713

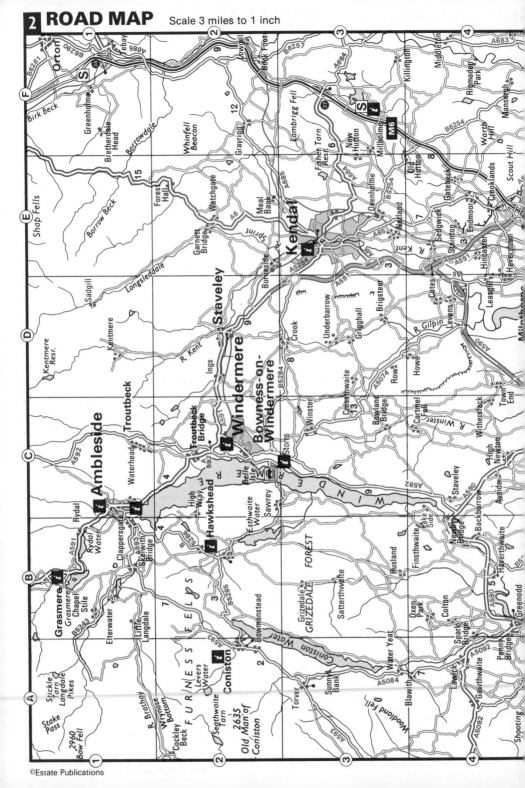

2 ROAD MAP Scale 3 miles to 1 inch

©Estate Publications

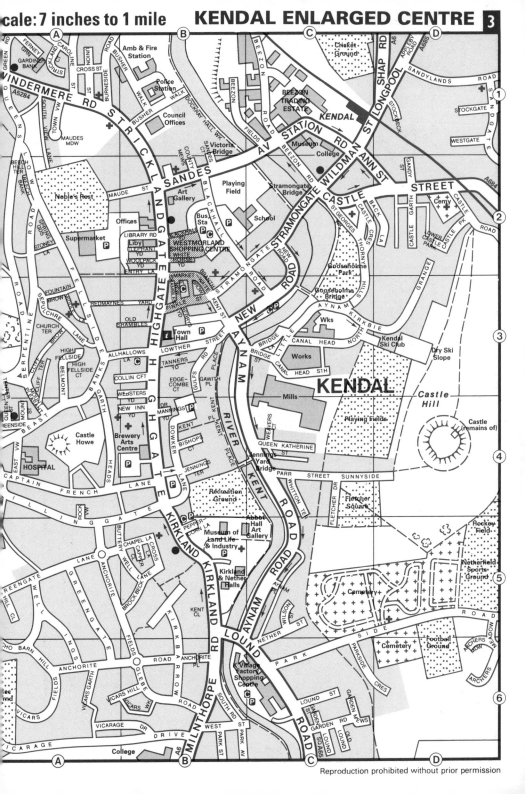

Scale: 7 inches to 1 mile

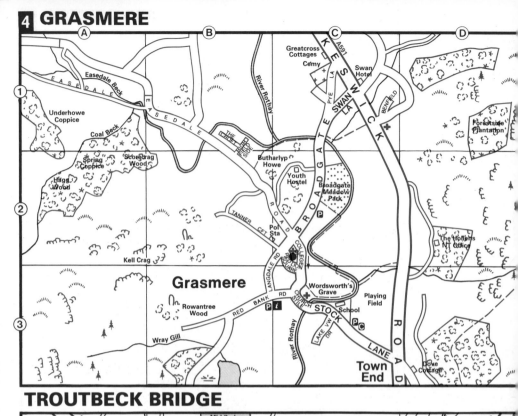

TROUTBECK BRIDGE

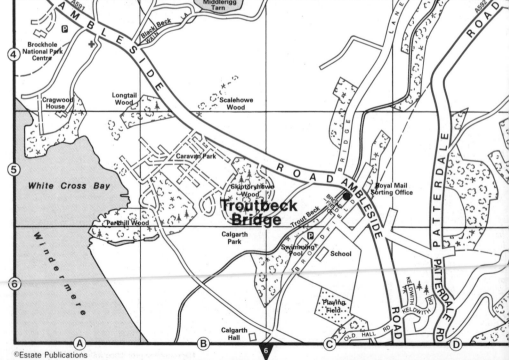

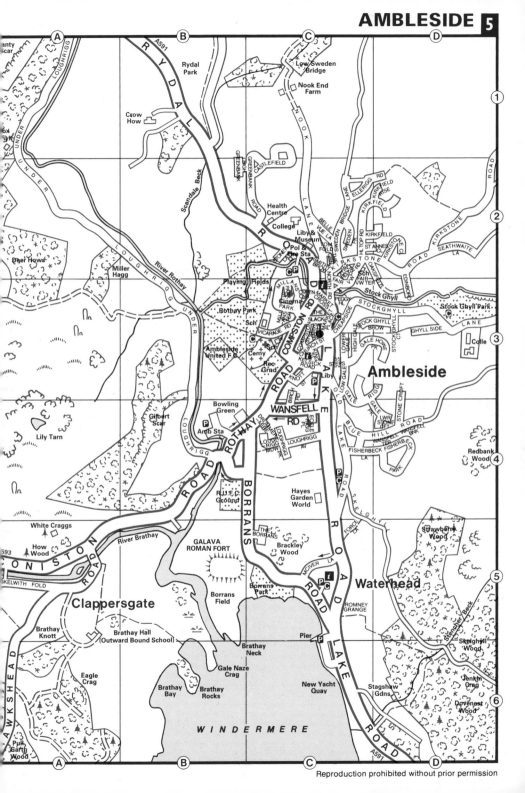

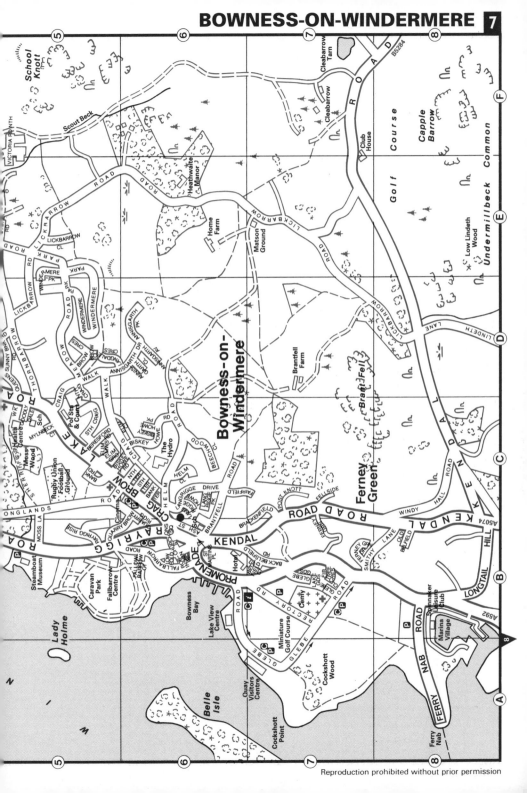

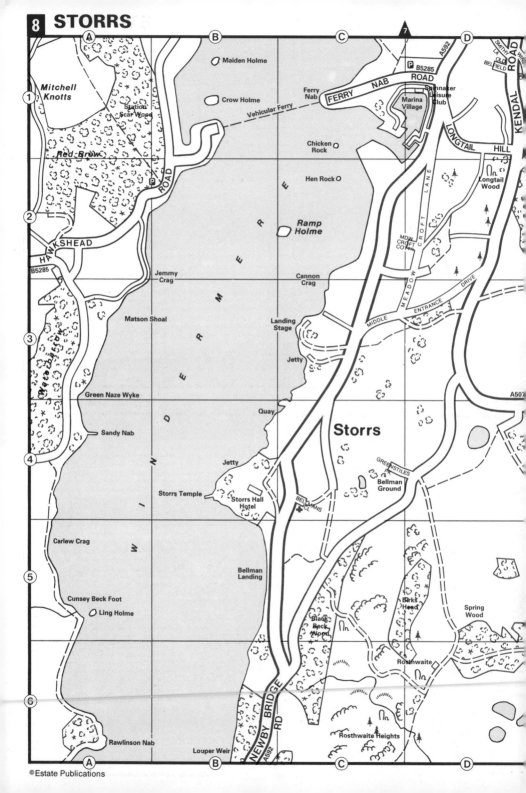

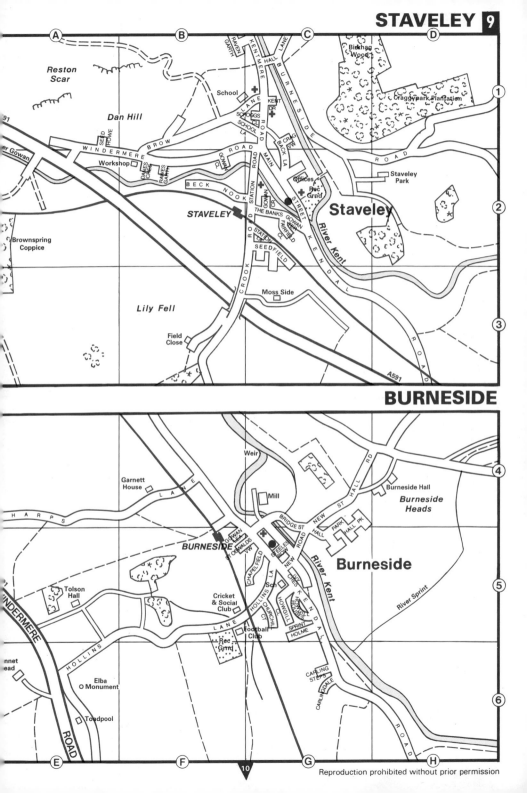

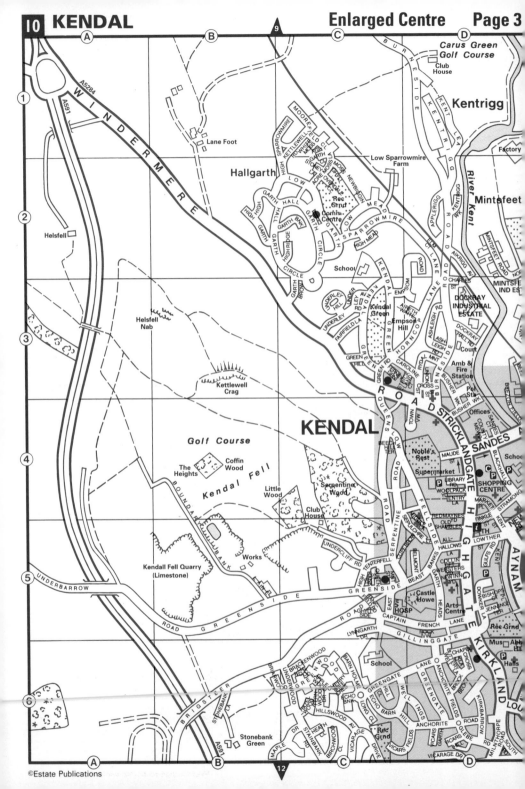

Carus Green
Golf Course
Club House

Kentrigg

Factory

Lane Foot

Hallgarth

Low Sparrowmire Farm

Mintsfeet

Helsfell

Rec Grnd

Corfin Centre

MINTSFEET IND ES

School

DOCKRAY INDUSTRIAL ESTATE

Helsfell Nab

Kendal Green

Empson Hill

Court

Amb & Fire Station

Kettlewell Crag

Pol Sta

Offices

KENDAL

SANDES

Golf Course

Noble's Rest

Supermarket

School

The Heights

Coffin Wood

SHOPPING CENTRE

Kendal Fell

Little Wood

Serpentine Wood

LIBRARY WOOLPACK YD ENTRY

Club House

REDMAYNES OLD'D SHAMBLES

ALL-HALLOWS

Kendall Fell Quarry (Limestone)

Works

UNDERCLIFF RD

TENTERFELL

NEWTOWN

UNDERBARROW

GREENSIDE

Castle Howe

HOSP

Arts Centre

Rec Grnd

ROAD

Mus

KIRKLAND

Halls

School

Stonebank Green

Rec Grnd

VICARAGE DR

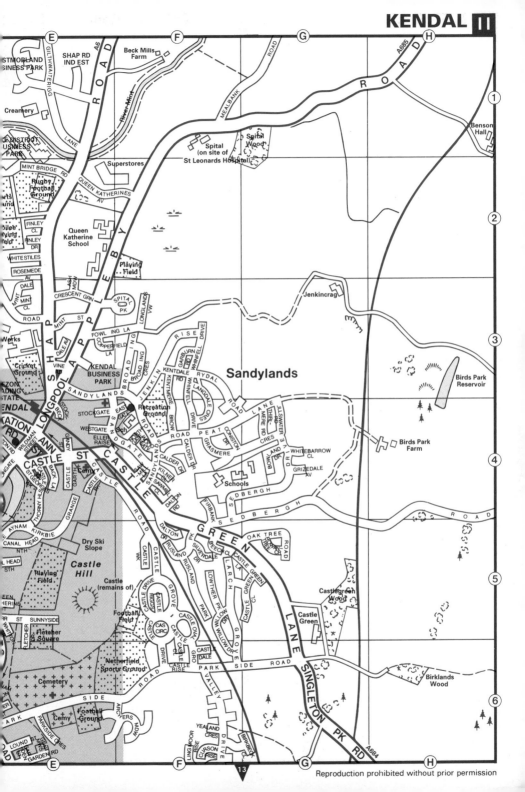

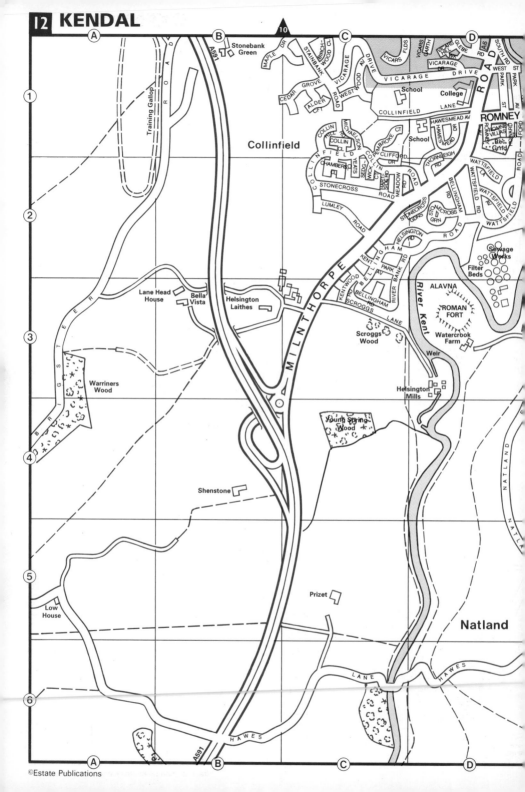

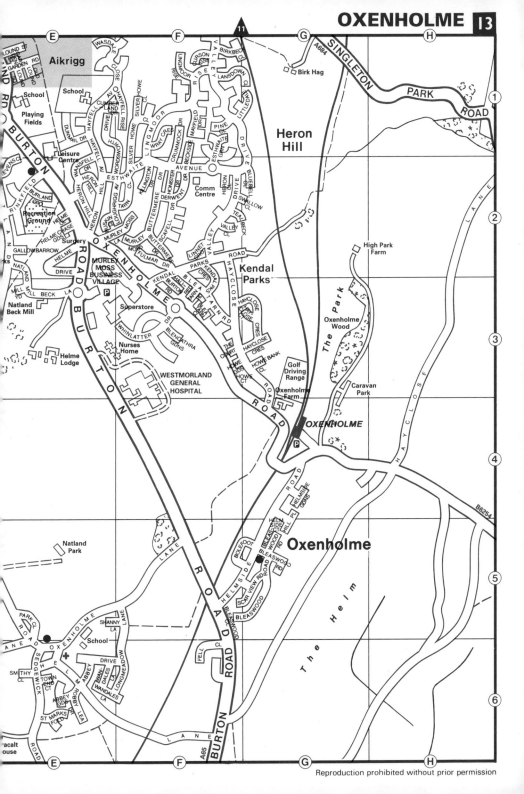

Aikrigg

Birk Hag

Heron Hill

School

School

Playing Fields

Leisure Centre

Recreation Ground

Surgery

GALLOWBARROW

Natland Beck Mill

MURLEY MOSS BUSINESS VILLAGE

Superstore

Whinlatter

Nurses Home

Helme Lodge

WESTMORLAND GENERAL HOSPITAL

Kendal Parks

High Park Farm

Oxenholme Wood

The Park

Golf Driving Range

Oxenholme Farm

Caravan Park

OXENHOLME

Natland Park

Oxenholme

The Helm

School

The Index includes some names for which there is insufficient space on the maps. These names are preceded by an * and are followed by the nearest adjoining thoroughfare.

AMBLESIDE

Belle Vue La. LA22	5 C2
Birch Rd. LA22	5 C4
Blue Hill Rd. LA22	5 C4
Borrans Rd. LA22	5 B4
*Bridge St,	
North Rd. LA22	5 C2
Castlefield. LA22	5 C2
Chapel Hill. LA22	5 C2
Cheapside. LA22	5 C3
Church St. LA22	5 C3
Compston Cnr. LA22	5 C3
Compston Rd. LA22	5 C3
Compston St. LA22	5 C3
Coniston Rd. LA22	5 A5
Drummermire. LA22	5 C4
Ecclerigg Pl. LA22	5 C4
Edinboro. LA22	5 D2
Ellerigg Rd. LA22	5 C2
Fair View Rd. LA22	5 C2
Fair View Ter. LA22	5 C2
55 Steps. LA22	5 C3
Fisherbeck La. LA22	5 C4
Fisherbeck Pk. LA22	5 D4
Force La. LA22	5 C5
Gale Howe Pk. LA22	5 C3
Gale Pk. LA22	5 C4
Gale Rigg. LA22	5 C3
Ghyll Side. LA22	5 D3
Greenbank Rd. LA22	5 C2
Hawkshead Rd. LA22	5 A6
High Gale. LA22	5 C3
High Greenbank. LA22	5 B2
Hill Top Rd. LA22	5 C2
How Head. LA22	5 C2
Kelsick Rd. LA22	5 C3
King St. LA22	5 C3
Kirkfield. LA22	5 C2
Kirkfield Rise. LA22	5 C2
Kirkstone Clo. LA22	5 D2
Kirkstone Rd. LA22	5 C2
Knott St. LA22	5 C3
Lake Rd. LA22	5 C3
Loughrigg Av. LA22	5 C4
Loughrigg Mdw. LA22	5 C4
Loughrigg Pk. LA22	5 C4
Low Gale. LA22	5 C3
Lower Gale. LA22	5 C3
Lower Stone Croft. LA22	5 D4
Market Cross. LA22	5 C3
Market Pl. LA22	5 C3
McIver La. LA22	5 C5
*Millans Ct,	
Millans Pk. LA22	5 C3
Millans Pk. LA22	5 C3
Millans Ter. LA22	5 C3
Nook La. LA22	5 C1
North Rd. LA22	5 C2
Oaksfield. LA22	5 C2
Old Lake Rd. LA22	5 C3
*Old Stamphouse Yd,	
Lake Rd. LA22	5 C3
Park St. LA22	5 C3

Peggy Hill. LA22	5 C3
*Pinfold Row,	
The Green. LA22	5 C2
Romney Grange. LA22	5 C5
Rothay Rd. LA22	5 B4
Rydal Rd. LA22	5 B1
St Annes Clo. LA22	5 C2
St Marys La. LA22	5 C3
Seathwaite La. LA22	5 D2
Skelghyll La. LA22	5 C4
Skelwith Fold. LA22	5 A5
Smithy Brow. LA22	5 C2
*Stock Ter,	
North Rd. LA22	5 C2
Stockghyll Brow. LA22	5 C3
Stockghyll Ct. LA22	5 D3
Stockghyll La. LA22	5 C3
Stone Croft. LA22	5 D4
Stoney La. LA22	5 C2
Sweden Bridge La. LA22	5 C2
Sweden Pk. LA22	5 C2
The Borrans. LA22	5 C5
*The Gale,	
Lower Gale. LA22	5 C3
The Green. LA22	5 C2
*The Lakelands,	
Lower Gale. LA22	5 C3
The Slack. LA22	5 C3
Tom Fold. LA22	5 C2
Under Loughrigg. LA22	5 B3
Vicarage Rd. LA22	5 C2
Wansfell Bank. LA22	5 D4
Wansfell Rd. LA22	5 C4
Wansfell Ter. LA22	5 D4

GRASMERE

Benfield. LA22	4 C1
Broadgate. LA22	4 C2
Church Stile. LA22	4 C3
College St. LA22	4 C2
Easedale. LA22	4 A1
Easedale Rd. LA22	4 B1
High Field Side. LA22	4 B1
Keswick Rd. LA22	4 C1
*Kirk Allans,	
Stock La. LA22	4 C3
Lake View Dri. LA22	4 C3
Langdale Rd. LA22	4 B3
Pye La. LA22	4 C1
Red Bank Rd. LA22	4 B3
Red Lion Sq. LA22	4 C2
Stock La. LA22	4 C3
Swan La. LA22	4 C1
Tanner Croft. LA22	4 B2
The Croft. LA22	4 B1

KENDAL

Abbey Dri. LA9	13 E6
Abbey Gdns. LA9	13 E6
Acre Moss La. LA9	10 C2
Aikrigg Av. LA9	10 D2
Airethwaite. LA9	10 C3
Alder Croft. LA9	12 C1
*Alderwood,	
Hazelwood. LA9	10 C6
Allhallows La. LA9	3 A3
Anchorite Fields. LA9	3 A5

Anchorite Pl. LA9	3 B6
Anchorite Rd. LA9	3 A6
Ann St. LA9	3 C2
Appleby Rd. LA9	11 E3
Applerigg. LA9	10 D2
Applewood. LA9	10 C6
Archers Mdw. LA9	11 F6
Ash Mdw. LA9	11 E3
Ashleigh Rd. LA9	10 D3
Aynam Pl. LA9	3 C5
Aynam Rd. LA9	3 B3
Aysgarth Clo. LA9	10 C1
Back La. LA9	3 C2
Bank St. LA9	10 C5
Bankfield Rd. LA9	10 C5
Barn Holme. LA9	10 C6
Beast Banks. LA9	3 A4
Beckside. LA9	13 F2
Beech Bank. LA9	3 A2
Beech Clo. LA9	11 F5
Beech Hill Ter. LA9	3 A2
Beezon Flds. LA9	3 B1
Beezon Rd. LA9	3 C1
Bellingham Rd. LA9	12 C3
Belmont. LA9	3 A3
*Belmont Brow,	
Belmont. LA9	3 A3
Berrys Yd. LA9	3 B3
Birchwood Clo. LA9	10 C6
Birkbeck Clo. LA9	13 F1
Bishops Ct. LA9	3 B4
Blackhall Rd. LA9	3 B2
Blackhall Yd. LA9	3 B2
Blea Tarn Clo. LA9	13 F3
Blea Tarn Rd. LA9	13 F3
Bleaswood Rd. LA9	13 F5
Blencathra Gdns. LA9	13 F3
Bluebell Clo. LA9	13 G2
Bolefoot. LA9	13 F5
Boundary Bank La. LA9	10 B4
Bowland Dri. LA9	11 G4
Brackenwood. LA9	10 C6
Branthwaite Brow. LA9	3 B3
Briarwood. LA9	10 B6
Bridge La. LA9	3 C3
Bridge St,	
Burneside. LA9	9 C4
Bridge St, Kendal. LA9	3 C3
Brigsteer Rd. LA9	10 B6
Broad Ing. LA9	11 F3
Broad Ing Cres. LA9	11 F3
Brockbeck. LA9	3 B5
Burland Gro. LA9	13 E2
Burneside Rd. LA9	10 C1
Burton Rd, Kendal. LA9	13 E1
Burton Rd,	
Oxenholme. LA9	13 F6
Busher Wk. LA9	3 A1
Buttermere Dri. LA9	13 F2
Buttery Well La. LA9	3 A5
Calder Dri. LA9	11 F4
Canal Head Nth. LA9	3 C3
Canal Head Sth. LA9	3 C3
Capper Clo. LA9	3 B5
Captain French La. LA9	3 A4
Carling Steps. LA9	9 C6
Carlingdale. LA9	9 C6
Caroline St. LA9	3 A1
Castle Circle. LA9	11 F5
Castle Clo. LA9	11 F6
Castle Cres. LA9	3 C2
Castle Dale. LA9	11 F6
Castle Dri. LA9	11 F5

Castle Garth. LA9	3 D?
Castle Grn Clo. LA9	11 G?
Castle Grn La. LA9	11 E
Castle Gro. LA9	11 F?
Castle Oval. LA9	11 F?
Castle Pk. LA9	3 D?
Castle Riggs. LA9	11 F
Castle Rise. LA9	11 F?
Castle Rd. LA9	11 E?
Castle St. LA9	3 C?
Castle Wk. LA9	11 F?
Cedar Gro. LA9	12 C
Chambers Clo. LA9	12 C
Chapel La. LA9	3 B?
Chapelfield. LA9	9 C?
Charles St. LA9	10 D
Cherry Tree Cres. LA9	10 C?
Church Ter. LA9	3 A?
Churchill Ct. LA9	9 C?
Cliff Brow. LA9	3 A?
Cliff Ter. LA9	3 A?
Clifford Dri. LA9	12 C
Collin Clo. LA9	12 C
Collin Croft. LA9	3 B
Collin Hill. LA9	12 C
Collin Rd. LA9	12 C
Collinfield. LA9	12 C
Collinfield La. LA9	12 C
Coniston Dri. LA9	11 F
Copperfield La. LA9	11 E
County Mews. LA9	3 B
Crescent Grn. LA9	11 E
Cross La. LA9	3 B
Cross St. LA9	3 A
Crummock Dri. LA9	13 F
Cumberland Dri. LA9	13 E
Curson Rise. LA9	13 F
Dale Av. LA9	11 E
Dalton Dri. LA9	11 F
Dalton Rd. LA9	11 F
Derwent Dri. LA9	13 F
Dockray Hall Rd. LA9	10 D
Dockray Hall Wk. LA9	3 B
Dr Mannings Yd. LA9	3 B
Dowker La. LA9	3 B
Dunmail Dri. LA9	13 E
East Gate. LA9	11 F
East Vw. LA9	3 A
Echo Bank. LA9	10 C
Echo Barn Hill. LA9	3 A
Edgecombe Ct. LA9	3 B
Elephant Yd. LA9	3 B
Eller Raise. LA9	11 E
Elm Ct. LA9	10 D
Empsom Rd. LA9	10 C
Entry La. LA9	3 B
Esthwaite Av. LA9	13 E
Esthwaite Grn. LA9	13 F
Fairfield La. LA9	10 C
Fell Clo. LA9	13 F
Ferney Grn. LA9	3 A
Fernwood Dri. LA9	10 C
Finkle St. LA9	3 B
Finley Clo. LA9	11 E
Finley Dri. LA9	11 E
Firbank. LA9	11 F
Fletcher Clo. LA9	3 C
Ford Ter. LA9	12 D
Fountain Brow. LA9	3 A
Fowl Ing La. LA9	11 E
Fulmar Dri. LA9	13 F
Galley Clo. LA9	13 F
Gallowbarrow. LA9	13 E

Gandy St. LA9	3 D2
Garburn Rd. LA9	11 F3
Garden Mews. LA9	3 C5
Garden Rd. LA9	3 C6
Garden St. LA9	3 C6
Gardiner Bank. LA9	3 A1
Garth Bank. LA9	10 C2
Garth Brow. LA9	10 C3
Garth Heads. LA9	3 A3
Gawith Pl. LA9	3 B3
Ghyll Side. LA9	10 C5
Gillinggate. LA9	3 A4
Gilthwaiterigg La. LA9	11 E1
Glebe Rd. LA9	3 B6
Gowan Lea. LA9	9 B5
Grasmere Cres. LA9	11 F4
Green Hill. LA9	10 C5
Green Rd. LA9	10 C3
Greengate. LA9	3 A5
Greengate La. LA9	3 A5
Greenside. LA9	10 B5
Greenwood. LA9	10 C6
Grizedale Av. LA9	11 G4
Gulfs Rd. LA9	3 B3
Haliburton Rd. LA9	13 F3
Hall Garth Circle. LA9	10 C2
Hall Park. LA9	9 C5
Hall Rd. LA9	9 C4
Hartside Rd. LA9	12 C2
Hawes La. LA9	12 B6
Hawesmead Av. LA9	12 D1
Hawesmead Dri. LA9	12 D1
Hayclose Ct. LA9	13 G3
Hayclose Cres. LA9	13 G3
Hayclose La. LA9	13 H4
Hayclose Rd. LA9	13 F2
Hayfell Av. LA9	13 E1
Hayfell Rise. LA9	13 F1
Heath Clo. LA9	10 C6
Helme Chase Gdns. LA9	13 E2
Helme Clo. LA9	13 E2
Helme Dri. LA9	13 E2
Helme La. LA9	13 E6
Helmside Ct. LA9	13 G5
Helmside Gdns. LA9	13 G6
Helmside Rd. LA9	13 F5
Helsington Rd. LA9	12 C2
Heron Clo. LA9	13 F2
Heron Hill. LA9	13 E2
High Fellside. LA9	3 A3
High Fellside Ct. LA9	3 A3
High Garth. LA9	10 B2
High Mead. LA9	10 C2
High Sparrowmire. LA9	10 C2
High Tenterfell. LA9	10 C5
*High Tenterfell Ct, High Tenterfell. LA9	10 C5
Highgate. LA9	3 B3
Highridge. LA9	10 C2
Hill Clo. LA9	3 A5
Hill Pl. LA9	13 G5
Hillswood Av. LA9	10 C6
Hollins La. LA9	9 A6
Honister Dri. LA9	13 F2
Horncop La. LA9	10 C3
Howard St. LA9	12 D1
Howe Bank Clo. LA9	13 G3
Howe Ct. LA9	13 F3
Howe Gdns. LA9	13 F3
Howgill Clo. LA9	9 C5
Howgill Houses. LA9	9 C5
INDUSTRIAL & RETAIL:	
Beezon Trading Est. LA9	3 C1
Dockray Ind Est. LA9	10 D3
Kendal Business Pk. LA9	11 E3
Lake District Business Pk. LA9	11 E1
Mintsfield. LA9	10 D3
Murley Moss Business Village. LA9	13 E2
Shap Rd Ind Est. LA9	11 E1
Village Factory Shopping Centre. LA9	3 B6
Westmorland Business Pk. LA9	11 E1
Westmorland Shopping Centre. LA9	3 B2
Ivy Cres. LA9	9 C5
Jenkin Rise. LA9	11 F3
Jennings Ter. LA9	3 B4
Kendal Grn. LA9	10 C3
Kendal Parks Cres. LA9	13 F2
Kendal Parks Rd. LA9	13 F3
Kendal Rd. LA9	9 C5
Kent Clo. LA9	3 B5
Kent Lea. LA9	10 D1
Kent Park Av. LA9	12 C2
Kent Pl. LA9	3 B4
Kent St. LA9	3 B3
Kentdale Rd. LA9	11 F3
Kentmere Brow. LA9	11 F3
Kentrigg Rd. LA9	10 D1
Kentrigg Wk. LA9	10 D2
Kentwood Rd. LA9	12 C3
*Kettlewell Clo, Kettlewell Rd. LA9	10 C1
Kettlewell Rd. LA9	10 C1
Killington Dri. LA9	13 F2
Kilner Clo. LA9	11 F4
Kirkbarrow. LA9	3 B5
Kirkbie Grange. LA9	3 C3
Kirkland. LA9	3 B5
Lansdown Clo. LA9	13 F1
Larch Gro. LA9	11 F5
Leaswood Clo. LA9	13 F5
Levens Clo. LA9	13 E2
Library Rd. LA9	3 B2
Lingmoor Rise. LA9	13 F1
Linnet Gro. LA9	13 F2
Little Aynam. LA9	3 C3
Littledale. LA9	13 G1
Long Clo. LA9	10 C6
Longlands Vw. LA9	11 F3
Longmeadow La. LA9	13 E6
Longpool. LA9	3 D1
Loughrigg Av. LA9	13 E2
Lound Rd. LA9	3 B5
Lound Sq. LA9	3 C6
Lound St. LA9	3 C6
Low Fellside. LA9	3 A1
Low Garth. LA9	10 C2
Low Mead. LA9	10 C2
Lower Castle Pk. LA9	3 D2
Lowther Pk. LA9	11 F5
Lowther St. LA9	3 B3
Lumley Rd. LA9	12 C2
Lynngarth Dri. LA9	10 C5
Maple Dri. LA9	10 B6
Market Pl. LA9	3 B3
Maude St. LA9	3 A2
Maudes Mdw. LA9	3 A1
Mayfield Dri. LA9	13 F1
Meadow Rd. LA9	12 C2
Mealbank Rd. LA9	11 F1
Michaelson Rd. LA9	12 C1
Mill Yd. LA9	13 E3
Milnthorpe Rd. LA9	12 C3
Mint Bridge Rd. LA9	11 E2
Mint Clo. LA9	11 E3
Mint Dale. LA9	11 E3
Mint St. LA9	11 E3
Mintsfeet Rd. LA9	10 D3
Mintsfeet Rd Nth. LA9	10 D2
Moorefield Clo. LA9	10 C1
Moss Ghyll. LA9	10 C2
Mount Pleasant. LA9	3 A3
Mount St. LA9	10 C5
Murley Moss. LA9	13 F2
Murley Moss La. LA9	13 E2
Natland Mill Beck La. LA9	13 E2
Natland Rd. LA9	13 E2
Nether St. LA9	3 C6
New Inn Yd. LA9	3 B4
New Rd, Burnside. LA9	9 C5
New Rd, Kendal. LA9	3 B3
New Shambles. LA9	3 B3
New St. LA9	9 C4
Newbiggin. LA9	10 B2
Northgate. LA9	11 F4
Oak Tree Rd. LA9	11 G5
Oak Wood. LA9	10 C6
Old Lound. LA9	3 C6
Old Shambles. LA9	3 B3
Overdale Ct. LA9	10 C2
Oxenholme La. LA9	13 E6
Oxenholme Rd. LA9	13 E2
Park Av. LA9	12 D1
Park Clo. LA9	13 E5
Park Side Rd. LA9	3 C6
Park St. LA9	12 D1
Parkside Cres. LA9	3 C6
Parr St. LA9	3 C4
Peat La. LA9	11 F4
Pembroke Ct. LA9	12 C1
Peppercorn La. LA9	3 B5
Pine Clo. LA9	13 F1
Queen Katherine St. LA9	3 C4
Queen Katherines Av. LA9	11 E2
Queen St. LA9	10 C5
Queens Rd. LA9	3 A1
Red Tarn Rd. LA9	13 F3
Redmaynes Yd. LA9	3 A3
Rinkfield. LA9	13 E2
*Rinteln Sq, Elephant Yd. LA9	3 B2
River Bank Rd. LA9	12 C3
Robby Lea Dri. LA9	13 E6
Rock Vw. LA9	3 A4
Romney Av. LA9	12 D1
Romney Gdns. LA9	12 D1
Romney Rd. LA9	12 D1
Romney Villas. LA9	12 D1
Rosemede Av. LA9	11 E2
Rowantree Cres. LA9	11 G5
Ruskin Clo. LA9	13 E2
Rusland Pk. LA9	11 F5
Rydal Mount. LA9	10 D3
Rydal Rd. LA9	11 F3
St Georges Wk. LA9	3 C2
St Marks Fold. LA9	13 E6
St Oswalds Vw. LA9	9 B5
Sandes Av. LA9	3 B2
Sandes Ct. LA9	3 B1
Sandgate. LA9	11 E4
Sandylands Rd. LA9	11 E3
Sawmill Clo. LA9	11 F4
Sawmill La. LA9	11 F4
Scafell Dri. LA9	13 F2
Scar View Rd. LA9	13 F5
Scroggs La. LA9	12 C3
Sedbergh Dri. LA9	11 F4
Sedbergh Rd. LA9	11 F4
Sedgewick Rd. LA9	13 E6
Sedgwick Ct. LA9	12 C2
Sepulchre La. LA9	3 A3
Serpentine Rd. LA9	3 A3
Shanny La. LA9	13 E5
Shap Rd. LA9	11 E3
Sharps La. LA9	9 A4
Silver Howe Clo. LA9	13 F1
Silverdale Dri. LA9	11 F5
Singleton Pk Rd. LA9	11 G6
Smithy Clo. LA9	13 E6
South Rd. LA9	3 B6
South View La. LA9	3 A1
Sparrowmire La. LA9	10 C2
Spital Pk. LA9	11 E3
*Spring Bank, Charles St. LA9	10 D3
Spring Gdns. LA9	3 A2
Sprint Holme. LA9	9 C5
Stainbank Rd. LA9	10 C6
Station Rd. LA9	3 C1
Steeles Row. LA9	9 C5
Stockbeck. LA9	3 D1
Stockgate. LA9	11 E4
Stonebank La. LA9	10 B6
Stonecross Gdns. LA9	12 D2
Stonecross Grn. LA9	12 D2
Stonecross Rd. LA9	12 C2
Stoney La, Hallgarth. LA9	10 C2
Stoney La, Kendal. LA9	3 A2
Stramongate. LA9	3 C2
Strickland Ct. LA9	3 A1
Stricklandgate. LA9	3 A1
*Summerhill Gdns, Greenside. LA9	3 A4
Sunnyside. LA9	3 C4
Swallow Clo. LA9	13 G2
Tanners Yd. LA9	3 B3
Tarn Clo. LA9	13 F2
Tealbeck. LA9	13 F2
Tenterfell Ct. LA9	3 A3
The Court. LA9	13 F3
Thirlmere Rd. LA9	11 G4
Thornleigh Rd. LA9	12 D2
Thorny Hills. LA9	3 C2
Town End Ct. LA9	13 E6
Town Vw. LA9	3 A1
Ullswater Rd. LA9	11 G4
Underbarrow Rd. LA9	10 A5
Undercliff Rd. LA9	10 C5
Underley Av. LA9	10 C3
Underley Hill. LA9	10 C3
Underley Rd. LA9	10 C3
Underwood. LA9	10 C6
Union St. LA9	3 A1
Valley Dri. LA9	13 F2
Vicarage Dri. LA9	3 A6
Vicars Flds. LA9	3 A6
Vicars Garth. LA9	3 A6
Vicars Hill. LA9	3 A6
Vicars Wk. LA9	3 B6
Vine Rd. LA9	11 E3
Wandales La. LA9	13 E6
Wansfell Dri. LA9	13 E2
Wasdale Clo. LA9	13 E1
Wattsfield Av. LA9	12 D2
Wattsfield La. LA9	12 D2
Wattsfield Rd. LA9	12 D2
Weavers Ct. LA9	3 C4
Websters Yd. LA9	3 B3
Well Ings. LA9	3 A5
West St. LA9	3 B6
Westgate. LA9	11 E4
Westwood Av. LA9	12 C1
Whinfell Dri. LA9	11 F3
Whinlatter Dri. LA9	13 F3
White Moss. LA9	10 C1
Whitebarrow Clo. LA9	11 G4
Whitehorse Yd. LA9	3 B2
Whitestiles. LA9	11 E2
Whitton Ter. LA9	3 C4

Wildman St. LA9 — 3 C2
Willow Dri. LA9 — 11 F5
Wilson St. LA9 — 3 C5
Windermere Rd, Burneside. LA9 — 9 A5
Windermere Rd, Kendal. LA9 — 10 A1
Woodgate. LA9 — 11 F4
Woolpack Yd. LA9 — 3 B2
Wordsworth Dri. LA9 — 13 E2
Wray Cres. LA9 — 13 F1
Yeats Clo. LA9 — 12 C2

STAVELEY

Back La. LA8 — 9 C1
Beck Nook. LA8 — 9 B2
Brow La. LA8 — 9 B1
Burneside Rd. LA8 — 9 C1
Crag Vw. LA8 — 9 C1
Crook Rd. LA8 — 9 B3
Danes Cres. LA8 — 9 B2
Fairfield Clo. LA8 — 9 C2
Gowan Clo. LA8 — 9 B2
Gowan Cres. LA8 — 9 C2
Gowan Ter. LA8 — 9 C2
Hall La. LA8 — 9 C1
Kendal Rd. LA8 — 9 C2
Kent Dri. LA8 — 9 C1
Kentmere Rd. LA8 — 9 C1
Main St. LA8 — 9 C2
Raven Garth. LA8 — 9 B1
Rawes Garth. LA8 — 9 B2
School La. LA8 — 9 B1
Scroggs Clo. LA8 — 9 C1
Seed Howe. LA8 — 9 A1
Seedfield. LA8 — 9 C2
Station La. LA8 — 9 C2
Station Rd. LA8 — 9 C2
*Station Yd, Station La. LA8 — 9 C2
The Banks. LA8 — 9 C2
Windermere Rd. LA8 — 9 A1

WINDERMERE

Alexandra Rd. LA23 — 6 D4
Ambleside Rd, Troutbeck Bridge. LA23 — 4 A4
Ambleside Rd, Windermere. LA23 — 6 C2
Annisgarth Av. LA23 — 7 D6
Annisgarth Clo. LA23 — 7 D6
Annisgarth Dri. LA23 — 7 D6
Annisgarth Pk. LA23 — 7 D6
Ash St. LA23 — 7 B6

Back Belsfield Rd. LA23 — 7 B7
Bank Rd. LA23 — 7 C5
Bank Ter. LA23 — 7 C6
Beech St. LA23 — 6 D3
Beechwood Clo. LA23 — 7 C6
Beemire La. LA23 — 6 C4
Bellmans Clo. LA23 — 8 C4
Belsfield Ct. LA23 — 7 B7
Beresford Rd. LA23 — 7 C5
Birch St. LA23 — 6 D3
Birkfield Rd. LA23 — 6 E4
Birthwaite Gdns. LA23 — 6 D4
Birthwaite Rd. LA23 — 6 C3
Biskey Howe Pk. LA23 — 7 C6
Biskey Howe Rd. LA23 — 7 C5
Bowfell Cres. LA23 — 6 E3
Brackenfield. LA23 — 7 B7
Brantfell Rd. LA23 — 7 B6
Bridge La. LA23 — 4 C5
Broad St. LA23 — 6 D3
Broadfield. LA23 — 4 C6
Broadfield Clo. LA23 — 4 C5
Brook Rd. LA23 — 6 D4
Brow Clo. LA23 — 7 D5
Brow Cres. LA23 — 7 D5
Chestnut Rd. LA23 — 6 D4
Church St, Bowness-on-Windermere. LA23 — 7 B6
Church St, Windermere. LA23 — 6 D3
Claife Av. LA23 — 6 E3
Claife Clo. LA23 — 6 E4
*College Ct, Main Rd. LA3 — 6 D3
*College Gate, Elleray Gdns. LA23 — 6 D3
College Rd. LA23 — 6 D3
Common Rd. LA23 — 6 F3
Cornbirthwaite Rd. LA23 — 6 C4
Crag Brow. LA23 — 7 C6
Craig Wk. LA23 — 7 C5
Crescent Rd. LA23 — 6 D3
Cross St. LA23 — 6 D3
*Cumbria Ct, College Rd. LA23 — 6 D3
Droomer Dri. LA23 — 6 E4
Droomer La. LA23 — 6 F4
Elim Ct. LA23 — 7 C6
Elim Gro. LA23 — 7 C5
Elim Mews. LA23 — 7 C5
Elleray Gdns. LA23 — 6 D3
Elleray Rd. LA23 — 6 D3
Ellerthwaite Rd. LA23 — 6 D4
Ellerthwaite Sq. LA23 — 6 D4
Fairfield. LA23 — 7 C6
Fairfield Rd. LA23 — 6 E4
Fallbarrow Ct. LA23 — 7 B6
Fallbarrow Rd. LA23 — 7 B6
Fellside. LA23 — 7 C7
Ferney Grn. LA23 — 7 B7

Ferney Grn Dri. LA23 — 7 B7
Ferry Nab Rd. LA23 — 7 A8
Firtree Cres. LA23 — 7 B7
Gable Mews. LA23 — 6 D3
Ghyll Clo. LA23 — 6 E4
Ghyll Rd. LA23 — 6 E4
Glebe Clo. LA23 — 7 B7
Glebe Gdns. LA23 — 7 B7
Glebe Rd. LA23 — 7 A7
Goodly Dale. LA23 — 7 C5
Greenstiles Pk. LA23 — 8 C4
Havelock Rd. LA23 — 6 D3
Hawkshead Rd. LA22 — 8 A2
Hazel St. LA23 — 6 D3
Helm Clo. LA23 — 7 C6
Helm Rd. LA23 — 7 C6
High St. LA23 — 6 D3
*Hodge How, Old Hall Rd. LA23 — 6 B2
Holly Rd. LA23 — 6 D4
*Holly Ter, Havelock Rd. LA23 — 6 D3
Keldwith Dri. LA23 — 6 C1
Keldwith Pk. LA23 — 6 C1
Kendal Rd. LA23 — 7 B6
Lake Gdns. LA23 — 7 B7
Lake Rd. LA23 — 7 D5
Lane Head. LA23 — 6 E4
Langdale Cres. LA23 — 7 D5
Langrigge Dri. LA23 — 7 C6
Langrigge Howe. LA23 — 7 C6
Langrigge Pk. LA23 — 7 C6
Lickbarrow Clo. LA23 — 7 E5
Lickbarrow Rd. LA23 — 7 D5
Limethwaite Rd. LA23 — 6 E4
Lindeth La. LA23 — 7 D8
Longlands Rd, Bowness-on-Windermere. LA23 — 7 C5
Longlands Rd, Windermere. LA23 — 6 C4
Longtail Hill. LA23 — 7 B8
Low Fold. LA23 — 7 B6
Main Rd. LA23 — 6 D3
Meadow Croft Cotts. LA23 — 8 C2
Meadow Croft La. LA23 — 8 C3
Meadow Rd. LA23 — 7 D5
Middle Entrance Dri. LA23 — 8 C3
Mill Brow. LA23 — 6 F4
Mill Rise. LA23 — 6 F4
Moss La. LA23 — 7 B5
Mylnegarth Gdns. LA23 — 6 E4
Nelson Rd. LA23 — 6 E4
New Rd. LA23 — 6 D4
Newby Bridge Rd. LA23 — 8 B6
North Craig. LA23 — 7 D5
North Ter. LA23 — 7 C6
Oak St. LA23 — 6 D3
Oaklands Dri. LA23 — 6 D2

Oakthwaite Rd. LA23 — 6 D
Old Belfield. LA23 — 7 B
Old College La. LA23 — 6 D
Old College Pk. LA23 — 6 D
Old Hall Rd. LA23 — 6 B
Oldfield Ct. LA23 — 6 D
Oldfield Rd. LA23 — 6 D
Orrest Dri. LA23 — 6 D
Park Av. LA23 — 6 D
Park Clo. LA23 — 6 D
Park Rd. LA23 — 6 E
Phoenix Way. LA23 — 6 D
Post Knott. LA23 — 7 C
Princes Rd. LA23 — 6 D
Priory Grange. LA23 — 6 C
Priory Mews. LA23 — 6 C
Promenade. LA23 — 7 B
Quarry Brow. LA23 — 7 B
Quarry Rigg. LA23 — 7 B
Queens Dri. LA23 — 7 D
Queens Sq. LA23 — 7 B
Rayrigg Gdns. LA23 — 6 D
Rayrigg Rise. LA23 — 7 B
Rayrigg Rd, Bowness-on-Windermere. LA23 — 7 B
Rayrigg Rd, Windermere. LA23 — 6 B
Rectory Rd. LA23 — 7 B
Robinson Pl. LA23 — 7 B
St Marks Pk. LA23 — 6 C
St Martins Pl. LA23 — 7 B
Salisbury Pl. LA23 — 6 D
School Knot Clo. LA23 — 6 E
School Knot Dri. LA23 — 6 E
Sherrifs Wk. LA23 — 7 C
Smithy La. LA23 — 7 B
South Craig. LA23 — 7 C
South Cres. LA23 — 6 C
South Ter. LA23 — 7 C
Spooner Vale. LA23 — 6 C
Springfield Rd. LA23 — 6 E
Sunny Bank Rd. LA23 — 7 D
The Hoo Dri. LA23 — 6 C
The Terrace. LA23 — 6 D
Thornbarrow Rd. LA23 — 7 D
Thornthwaite Rd. LA23 — 6 E
Thwaites La. LA23 — 6 E
Upper Oak St. LA23 — 6 E
Victoria Rd. LA23 — 7 E
Victoria Rd Nth. LA23 — 7 E
Victoria St. LA23 — 6 D
Wain La. LA23 — 4 E
West Cres. LA23 — 6 D
Whinfield Rd. LA23 — 6 D
Windermere Pk. LA23 — 7 D
Windy Hall Rd. LA23 — 7 C
Woodland Clo. LA23 — 6 E
Woodland Rd. LA23 — 6 D
Wynlass Pk. LA23 — 6 C